Hindsight is f/20

*Lessons from my ten years as a
photo studio owner*

By Maureen Cogan

To all the photographers who so unselfishly taught me what they know.

I should have listened.

"Some of us learn from other people's mistakes and the rest of us have to be the other people."

— Zig Ziglar

Table of Contents

Introduction

While I had a great time in my photography business, I chose one of the worst days to launch it. That Monday morning I sent the e-mail (that I had spent hours writing to get just right) to my family and friends. It announced that I was so excited to be starting a photography business and there was a special offer for a free session and an 8x10. The next morning was September 11, 2001 and filled with news of the towers coming down.

Understandably, no one paid any attention to my little e-mail. That wasn't a mistake, of course, but an accident of timing. What followed, though, was ten years of my learning how to run a business the hard way—by doing things wrong and paying the price.

This book is what I learned in the ten years between that e-mail and the day I took what I call a "regular" job because it has a "regular" paycheck. I'm no business expert, but one of the most frustrating things about looking back on my time as a portrait studio owner is that hindsight is 20/20. I can clearly see all the things I did wrong that I couldn't see when I was in the thick of things.

If you're just beginning your photography career, you will learn a lot from this book. And not the hard way like I did. If you're an established professional, you may see some of the same mistakes in this book you are making and be able to correct them before you consider taking a "regular" job, too.

The business began when my neighbors and friends started asking me to take their graduation and family portraits, which was in 1999 after I earned my diploma from the New York Institute of Photography. It's a correspondence school and it was perfect for me because at that time I had an infant and a husband who traveled all week and only came home on weekends. The program was very detailed and comprehensive and covered portraits, landscape, bridal, high fashion, journalism, product, and architecture photography. I received books and tests and was given photo assignments. I then took pictures and mailed them (no e-mail then) to my instructor who mailed back critiques and a score on a cassette tape (remember those?). So over the two years it took to finish the course, I asked my neighbors and friends to be models for my assignments. After a while they began asking me to take portraits for them. The business grew from there.

It was great for ten years until I realized that I am a good photographer but a bad business owner. If you're reading this book, I assume you are already a good photographer. Here is how you can be a great photo business owner, too.

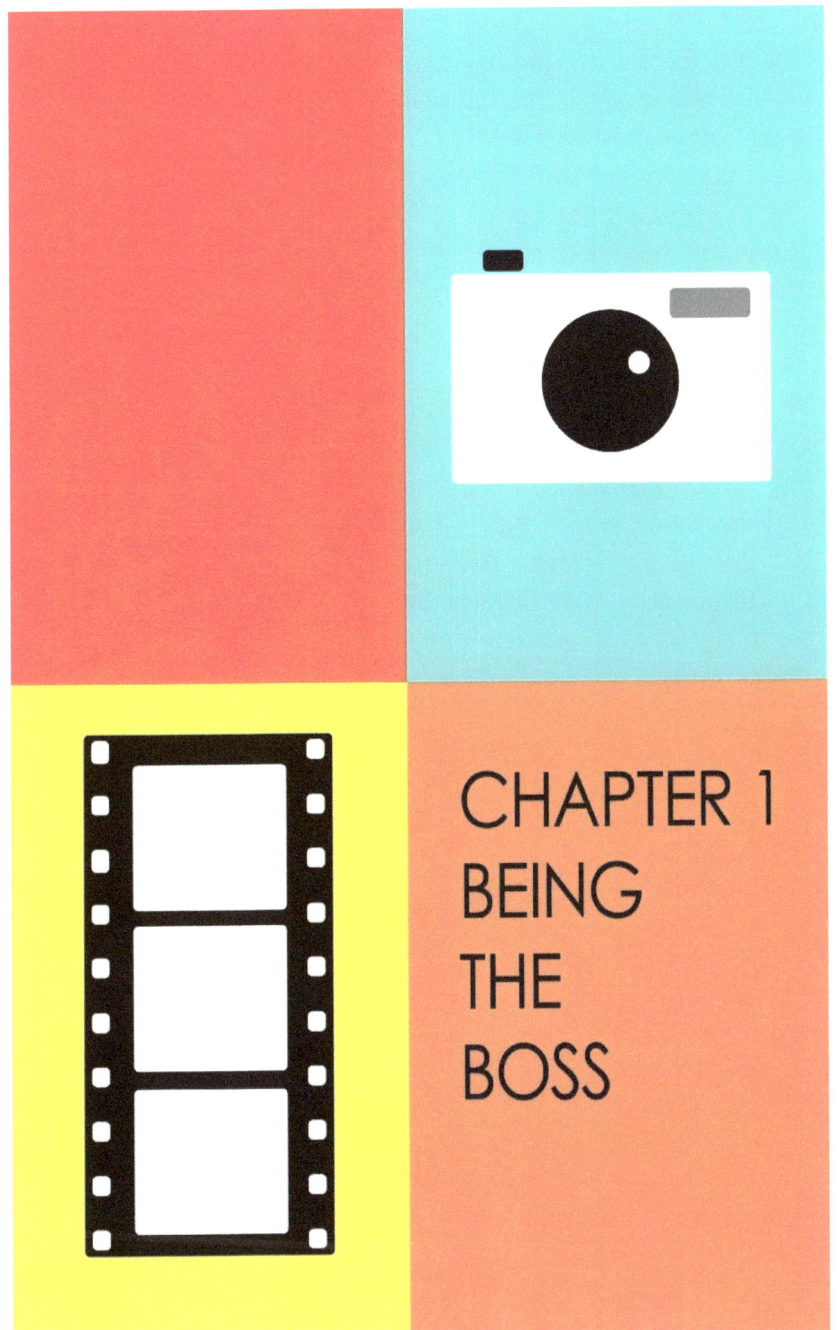

CHAPTER 1
BEING
THE
BOSS

"I don't think I had the right kind of self-confidence for such a creative industry. I was sure of my business skills, but not as sure of my vision. I wish I had trusted that more. I learned a lot more from friendships with other photographers than I ever did from photography organizations. I think you need to study and know what you are doing, but from there I think associations with others who have been where you want to go are invaluable.

So many people are afraid to talk to other photographers, afraid they will let go of a secret they think they have and help the competition. I never thought of other photographers as competition in that way. Perhaps as the field narrows they are, but we are mostly competing with other industries for those dollars. We needed to let our customers know why spending their money on photographs that were professionally done and would last a lifetime was more important than buying another new gadget for themselves.

I'm not sure we've done that very well as an industry and I certainly failed to be able to do that as an individual photographer."
–Sara Steger, Owner M&S Photography, Callao, Virginia

You Are the Boss
It sounds easy, but it's sometimes hard to do: Remember that it's your business and you are the boss. It's a mistake to think the client is the boss. I started out thinking this and so I felt stressed around clients because I never knew what they were going to ask for. Once I got over this, I was a better business person. I'm not saying never go out of your way to make someone happy. I'm saying have a limit to how far you will go and stick to it.

I understand the reason for the saying "the customer is always right." It's saying if you treat clients well, they will return to you and refer people to you. But there are a few people who use this mantra to get what they want even when it's totally unreasonable. Once I realized that, I had answers ready for unreasonable requests and was better able to counter them with compromises that made me and the client happy. If you let a client run over you and take advantage of you, guess what kind of referrals you're going to get from them? People who are just like them and expect the same treatment. And you're going to lose money and feel cheated and stressed.

Associations

Join associations, even small local ones. If there isn't one, start one. My local association was 45 minutes away and met at 6:00 in the evening. As a mom with small children, this was the worst time of day to meet. In order to get there by 6:00, I left at 5:15 after picking up the kids from school at 4:00. So dinner was rushed for the kids and sometimes I didn't get any and then the drive was during rush hour so the traffic was terrible. Although I liked the group and continued to attend here and there, I started my own group in the town I live in and we met during the day. Several people joined and it was very rewarding.

Along with the camaraderie of being around other photographers, association membership elevated my work because I talked with other members about what they were doing and it inspired me and made me see what great things regular people can do. It also created some friendly competition, which made me work a little better.

Also, consider joining a group outside of photography as well. I belonged to a photographers' association in Annapolis, Professional Photographers of America (PPA), plus an association for stay-at-home moms who owned their own businesses. I liked all these groups equally because the photographers at that time were mostly men and while they were very nice people who I very much enjoyed talking with, they had no idea what my daily life was like as a mom juggling kids, company, clients, husband, home, pet, etc. On the other hand, the moms group couldn't talk with me about photography but they understood exactly what my day-to-day life was like and could talk about that and offer support and advice. The members of the non-photography group will identify with different aspects of you and what you are going through.

Get it in Writing
If you arrive at a session location and the arrangement isn't what you had agreed to before the session, speak up right away. Have it in writing in a contract or e-mail and bring it to the client's attention that this is different than what you spoke about and charge for that. If I had kept this in mind instead of thinking, "the customer is always right," I would not have had such a bad experience with the incredible expanding family. Here's how it went.

I was contacted by a client whose extended family was coming to town and she wanted portraits of the kids–nieces, nephews, cousins. So I arranged a nice place to take the portraits at an old mansion and we set a date. The date came and it turned into a mob scene of the incredible expanding family. The session was supposed to be eight or so kids. But about 20 family members showed up all wanting their separate family groups taken. They had all decided spur of the moment to go ahead and have their portraits taken as well and were all dressed alike. So they had planned it. But no one had told me.

As a result of this and the fact that I didn't speak up, it took way longer than planned. I ran out of room on my memory card and was in the corner deleting bad images to make room. Then a family member showed up who couldn't climb the stairs so we all went outside in 30 degree weather to take a huge family portrait on the front steps of the mansion. I was unprepared for all of this but did my best because I had heard that the customer is always right and didn't want to seem inflexible.

Make It Worth It
At some point in your photography career you may want to drop or add services and raise prices. When you do so, you may lose clients. Although that can be scary, it's OK because you are changing something you don't want to do anymore and the only clients you'll lose are those who don't like the change. In the very beginning of my business I did not have a studio, so I traveled to my clients' homes to take portraits. I loaded all my equipment in the car, drove it to the client and set it up there. Clients, of course, loved this, especially ones with small children.

During this time, I photographed a family who lived several miles away and had two kids. The kids ran the house. There was absolutely no parental control or discipline going on at all and the result was chaos and lots of stress. Plus there was an untrained dog running around that made it even more stressful. Miraculously, I captured some good portraits, but the experience took so long and was so stressful that on the way home in the car I actually considered not photographing children anymore.

When this family called again a couple of years later, I had a studio and only traveled to clients' homes for a premium price. I told them the new situation and quoted them the premium session fee to come to their home. They lived pretty far away from me, and I had done it the first time because it was the beginning of my career and I was doing anything to get work and referrals. But two years later, I was trying to get away from traveling. They were so angry, they sent me a nasty e-mail with rude language about how unfair it was to charge them that much to come to their home and they said forget it, they didn't want me to take the pictures anyway. This response cemented in my mind that they weren't the kind of people I wanted to work with and I was happy that I didn't have to. If they had agreed, I would have put on my "I'm a professional" hat and done a great job for them. And the extra money would have made it worth it. Since they didn't, I was just as happy not to have to deal with them again.

If you're going to offer a service because the clients want it but you don't like providing it (like traveling), make the price high enough that it will be worth the hassle.

This happened another time with a client who came to my studio. Their child was so unruly I didn't want to ever have to deal with her again. When they called three years later, I told them I had restructured my business and the prices were much higher. By the way, I did lose a couple of clients when I did so, but it was OK since I didn't want to work for the lower price anymore. I quoted them the new, higher price and they agreed right away. I was disappointed that I was going to work with them again, but the extra income made up for it and they were happy with their portraits.

Get a Deposit
I can't believe it took me so long to realize this one. When a client makes an appointment to come in for a session, get a deposit. The fee holds their space in your schedule. I can't even tell you what a big difference this makes. When clients don't pay for a session in advance, they rarely show up. I know because I didn't require one for a while after I opened my business and there were lots and lots of no-shows. Some didn't even call to say they weren't coming. Once I began charging a fee—it wasn't even that much, clients began arriving for their sessions without fail.

I used to do this day of sessions promotion where I would rent space at a local community center and schedule sessions all day long about 45 minutes apart. This let me keep the session fee low, see lots of people (in theory) and earn the real money later when they saw the proofs. I paid for the space up front myself and hoped to make it back in session fees that day so at least the space was paid for and I didn't lose anything. I then took appointments via e-mail and over the phone without a deposit. What happened is that I sat there all day and maybe three people showed up. I sat there all day and what I made in session fees didn't even pay for the modest fee I was paying for space. My cell phone would start ringing in the morning and people would call to cancel for various reasons or some just didn't show up. And since I only photographed three clients, I made some profit when they saw their portraits and purchased prints, but it didn't make up for all the time setting up, breaking down, and being there all day. Once I began charging a very modest $25 just to hold the appointment time, no one cancelled.

Stay Current

Keep up with technology and upgrade your equipment and software as much as you can. Learn about new techniques, equipment, and processes. Now I know many of you reading this book are techies and will have no problem with this. But I'm not a technical person and don't really enjoy the research and learning curve that it takes to keep up with changes and purchase new equipment and computers.

I know that many photographers love technical things and gadgets. Taking a little side trip, I once spoke at a local camera club about props and posing. I brought a bunch of props and had a slideshow that ran with my presentation. It showed the portraits that resulted from using the various props, stools and loveseats I was showing. I even had a model there to show all the different ways clients could be posed on the different pieces of furniture with the props. There was one picture where the camera was pulled back enough that my light stand and light were showing in the picture. I didn't bother to crop it out because I wasn't showing it to a client.

The camera club members jumped on that picture. A voice shouted out in the middle of my presentation, "What kind of light is that?" This began a whole discussion on equipment. I couldn't believe it! They didn't want to hear about posing and props, they wanted to know all about my lights, diffusers, flash units, camera, tripod (which, I have to admit, is a pretty sweet Manfrotto pistol grip, ball head version) and background stands. I had to go with it. That's what they wanted to talk about.

But if you're like me and don't enjoy the technical part of photography, it will benefit you to force yourself to learn about new technology and software. Since I don't enjoy research, I did it mainly by talking with other photographers to see what they liked and then trying it myself. I read *Professional Photographer*, *Rangefinder*, and *Popular Photography* to see what was new. It is imperative to at least know what's going on even if you don't use the most up-to-date equipment. Have a good reason to buy something and don't buy it just because it's new and cool. I know this is hard for technical types and if you have the money, go for it. But you can go broke trying to have the newest of everything since things change so fast. If you don't need it and it won't pay for itself in jobs that you get because you have it, try to resist the urge to buy it.

For example, in my business I never used the full version of Photoshop. I always used Elements. The reason is that I never had a retouching task that I thought, "Oh, I wish I had the full version so I could (insert task here.)" I did update the version of Elements every so often, though. I purchased a new camera only when I reached a point where I was having trouble with something such as getting good high-resolution portraits of large groups. That's when I purchased a new camera and upgraded my lens knowing that the group portraits I took would be that much better and I would earn more because I had that equipment.

Purchase only things you need, but keep up on what's available and be aware of when you may need to upgrade.

Some Clients Will Spend More Than You Would
I made the mistake of assuming that my clients wouldn't purchase anything I wouldn't purchase. I assumed that my clients could not afford the things I could not afford. I was wrong. Many of my clients were more affluent than me and they were asking for framing, albums, jewelry and other things I did not offer because I thought they were too pricey. Don't assume anything. Carry items in all price ranges and some clients will spend extra on the higher priced items.

Give Clients Guidance
Be specific in letting clients know how to use the digital images you take for them. I took many executive portraits and once took a woman's portrait for a book jacket. I assumed since she'd penned a book, she knew how to handle copyright and credit. I was wrong. That photo appeared on every copy of her book and I was not credited with it once anywhere in the book. She went on to use it on her business cards, website, and blog page without any credit to me. Now this was before we photographers had a good handle on how to charge for and monitor digital files so I didn't really know what I was doing either. But all you have to do is look at any professionally published book and you'll find the photo credit near the portrait or inside the first few pages somewhere. I thought everyone knew this.

From then on, when I delivered a retouched, high resolution digital image to a client for print use on a book jacket, brochure, or article, I included instructions on how to credit me.

Be Your Personal Best

Compare your work to your own previous work. Don't think you're not a good photographer because you're not as good as Ansel Adams. I held myself up to photographers I admired and therefore, thought I was not good because I wasn't as good as they were. Don't compare yourself to other people too much. It's OK to have a mentor or someone you want to be like, but people have completely different circumstances, family situations, financial means, personalities, etc. and some people just have an easier time than you will for whatever reason. They may learn faster, become better faster, earn more, or have a nicer studio.

None of that matters.

What matters is: Are YOU better today than you were yesterday? Are YOU doing things to improve your photography and your business?

There's no excuse not to do your best or put forth an effort to do something really well. If you admire another photographer, strive to be as good as them or better. If you admire a studio's decor but don't have the means financially to do it the same way, find your own way to make your studio nice with your own budget and personal touches. Put forth some effort to paint some furniture, hang some curtains, and look for creative ways to improve your own situation. Make your studio the best you can and work on your photography techniques and don't compare it to someone else's or apologize for yours to other people.

Change is Coming

Change is inevitable, so roll with it as it comes down the pike. The industry is constantly changing and will continue to change. Products will change. Your favorite lab will change its policies or process. Leave if you must, but try it first. I saw some labs go out of business when things went from film to digital because they resisted the change and couldn't keep up. The labs that flourished had a period of hard work, new software with lots of bugs and periods of teaching clients how to use the software, but they are now in the forefront of their industry.

Re-Touch, But Gently

I learned to retouch two or three years into my business, which was late. There are so many great books out there that teach exactly what to do in Photoshop to retouch your images. My favorite books on this subject are the ones by Scott Kelby (I've never met Scott and am getting no fees for this). I took one class sponsored by the local PPA and also purchased Scott's PS Elements book. That book stays next to my computer always. It's completely dog eared and I've put tabs on about half the pages and labeled them to help me find what I'm looking for. I referred to it constantly in the beginning until I learned how to do all the retouching by memory. The books are great because they tell you step by step just what to do and include screenshots of the menus and what your screen will look like at each step. I highly recommend Kelby's books for beginning retouchers.

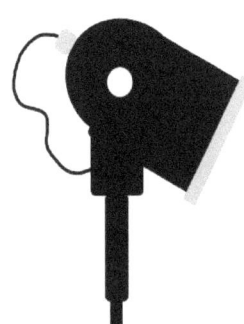

CLOSE UP

While we're on the subject, when retouching, keep it real. I see a lot of over-retouched images out there and a lot of teenage girls who look like mannequins. A standard retouch for me was to brighten the eyes a little, whiten the teeth but just enough to take out any yellow, and soften lines and wrinkles—soften, not erase. On teens, I also cut down on shine and erased blemishes (never erase a birthmark or freckles unless the client asks you to). Even though I was pretty light handed on the retouching, I did have one client get really angry and want them reprinted without any retouching. But most clients appreciate a little softening of their flaws.

Of course if the image needs it, eliminate a stray hair going across a face or a flipped up lapel. But try to keep the image as real as possible. See Chapter 6 for my favorite re-touching software.

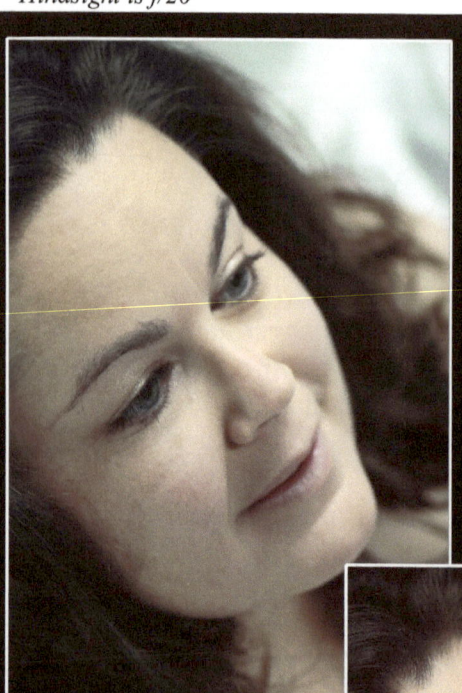

Original Image

Color corrected,
skin softening
filter applied.

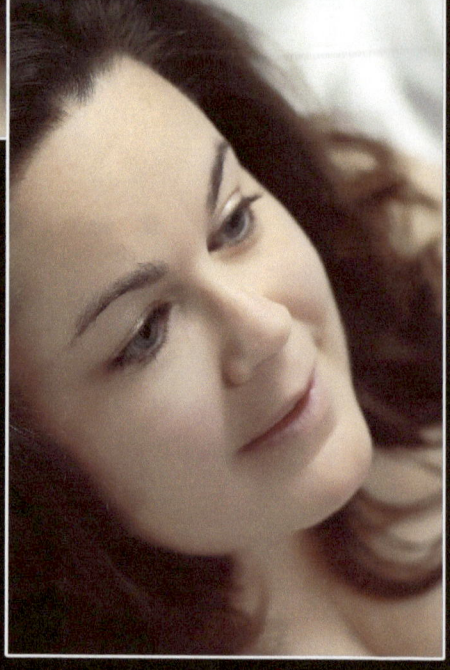

These show how just a little retouching can
elevate a photo to a professional portrait.

CHAPTER 2
MARKETING

"I started my first studio in my hometown when I was 21. I built a pretty large client base, but lost a lot of money and eventually had to close up shop. My biggest mistake was not learning about business and marketing before I started the studio. I learned the hard way, and today I have a reasonably successful studio. Aspiring photographers often ask me what they should do to become a professional and I tell them to study business and marketing first. If they find they like that aspect of this challenging profession, they should then study photography and improve those skills. If the business part doesn't interest them, it might be better to keep photography as a hobby. Otherwise they risk turning something they enjoy into just another job."
–David Anderson, Cr. Photog. CPP,
Owner, David Anderson Photography, Annapolis, Maryland

I really wish I had known David Anderson before I started my business. My biggest mistake was not knowing business or marketing. I didn't see the need to advertise. I thought I could have a word-of-mouth business. And I did, but I never had as many clients as I wanted. The small ads I did run were in high school play programs, preschool calendars, and community coupon books. The problem was that they didn't have a wide enough audience. Clients came in here and there, but not in a steady way. The way to get clients in the door is to advertise. Do a little research in your area and talk to other photographers to figure out what has worked for them. In some communities direct mail works really well. In others, displays at malls are the way to go. Look at successful photographers in your area and see where they are advertising. Then advertise in similar places.

Pay special attention to social media for your advertising. It's not that expensive and you can reach lots of people and also target your advertising to parents, high school seniors, or couples with new babies. Facebook, Twitter, and Google Ads are all avenues to look into. There are lots of online tutorials on how to use these if you don't know where to start.

Let Your Clients Advertise for You

After the proof appointment, give your client three or four of their favorite images as low-resolution files to post on social media sites. They are excited about them and want to show them off, so they'll do some promotion for you.

The Package Predicament

When I first started out, I offered some basic packages and my first few clients didn't like them. They all wanted to substitute sizes and swap things out for other things. I wasn't ready to answer their questions about swapping so I ended up giving them what they wanted and losing money since the package price was lower than the a-la-carte price. So I got rid of the packages and sold a-la-carte only from then on. This was a big mistake on my part. What happened is that clients would order 10 poses in 4x6 and I'd end up retouching 10 poses for a very small amount of money. By the way, I figured out that 4x6 is way too small to offer clients and stopped offering that size altogether.

The point of packages is to make it easy for you and your client. You sell the package with limited poses so you do minimal retouching but sell lots of prints and the client gets a few choices that won't overwhelm. Packages are the best way to do less retouching or get paid for the extra work. I also found that clients WANT packages because it makes it easier for them to choose what to purchase. It's too daunting to be faced with a bunch of proofs they love as well as an a-la-carte menu of different sizes and add-on products.

The trick is to put together packages with the most popular items and stand by them. Decide whether you will allow clients to swap out things for other things and have a plan for what you'll say and how much you'll charge for the swap so you're not stuck making a decision on the fly. Have packages in all price ranges and limit the number of poses in each. Then offer a few a-la-carte items they can add on. For example, offer an add-on of a few wallets or one 5x7 and price it higher so if they do order one 5x7 of that pose, you're compensated for the extra work to retouch another pose.

I also remember something from a photographer named Charles Lewis who recommended having a whopper package. The whopper package is something so luxurious and expensive that probably no one will purchase it. It includes higher priced items such as a silver locket with portraits in it, for example, a bunch of prints, an iPad with the images from the session loaded on it, and a framed 20x24 canvas. His theory was that even though very few clients will purchase the package (if any), it makes the other packages look better.

Social Media
Learn about social media and how to use it. If you're under the age of 30 or so, feel free to skip this section since you are the same age as the person I would hire to take over my social media tasks. If you're over the age of 30 or so, you may be reluctant to do this but it is a must. This is how people find photographers now. If clients like your photos, they will post them on their Facebook pages to share with all their friends. I was

slow at the gate to learn this and it cost me. It's a good idea to give high school seniors, for example, low-resolution files of their favorite poses to post online. If you don't they are going to scan them and post them anyway. I learned that one the hard way.

Make social media your friend. Make sure your website will appear attractive on a computer, phone, or tablet. If you don't know how, hire someone. High school seniors are great at this and many colleges offer classes on it, so if you're not good at it, like I wasn't, find a way to learn at least the basics. This is the way people communicate and it's an excellent venue for your images.

Be Your Own Congratulations Committee

Save examples of all your work that gets published anywhere. I was published a few times in *Professional Photographer* magazine and the British magazine *Engineering and Technology* and I never said anything to my clients! I was taught to be modest and not brag. But any time you are published anywhere, it's important and it should be talked about.

If you take an author's portrait for a book cover or book back (which I did several times), get a copy from them or purchase a copy, have them sign it, and keep it. Announce it on your website, your newsletter, and your Facebook page and display the book in your studio. I never did this and I kick myself now for not making a bigger deal out of it. In business, you have to brag and let people know about your accomplishments, otherwise how will they know? There's no Congratulations Committee marching around telling people for you. There are ways to announce your accomplishments without being arrogant.

Conventions Are Valuable

Attend conventions. Conventions are wonderful things. People may say they are just an excuse to go somewhere warm for a mini vacation. And you will go someplace warm and pretty, but you'll also learn what's new, meet people from all over the nation, attend classes and yes, have a little fun. The energy at a convention is fantastic. I only attended one and I wish I had attended more. I talked with other photographers and they wanted to talk. No one at home ever wanted to talk about photography with me, so this was wonderful! Photographers are a nice group of people, so by the time I got home I felt energized and ready to try new things. I highly recommend attending at least one convention each year. If you are a PPA member, your local chapter may host local or state conventions. Yea!

Annual Promotional Events

If you start an annual event such as a holiday session or spring park session, keep with it. The first two or three years may be sparse. Don't give up! As people learn of it, it will get more attention. I hosted a holiday portrait day each year on the first Saturday in November. I played holiday music, had cookies and juice, and lots of new holiday props. I scheduled people to come in from 10 am to 3 pm. I had some clients come in, but it was never full and I got discouraged and stopped doing it.

Looking back, I realize one of the problems was that it was too early. I live in Maryland, so the first weekend in November is often hot. One year it was 80 degrees that day. I'm not kidding. One year the first Saturday in November was November 1, the day after Halloween. Who wants to think about Christmas portraits the day after Halloween? The first weekend in December or the day after Thanksgiving would have been a better day.

But I am getting off the subject. A friend who owns a business doing custom embroidery began hosting a holiday show each year during the first weekend of November (yes, the same weekend as mine that I gave up on) to try to boost holiday sales and get orders in early for the holiday season. She hosts the event in her home and invites clients and friends. The first year, she served a few snacks and few of us showed up and bought some stuff. She's now in her eighth year of this and her entire sunroom is filled with a buffet of lunch and dinner food and she gets so many orders she can hardly handle them. She is actually contemplating not doing it anymore because even though she farms some of the work out to other embroiderers, she still can't handle the amount of work and have it ready by Christmas. Kind of a nice problem to have, huh?

The point is, when you begin an event that you want to be yearly, be prepared to wait two or three years before it really gets rolling. More and more people will find out about it every year that you do it and it will fill up. If your event fills up the first year, way to go!

Know Your Niche

Know what type of photographer you are. Some are very trendy and have the latest props, lighting gimmicks, and backgrounds. Some are classic and stick with plain backgrounds and classic lighting. Most mix the two depending on the client they are photographing that day. What I found is that the people who came to me wanted classic, even the seniors. But I kept trying the trendy things because I wanted to be trendy. I should have just stuck with the classics. It would have saved me time, money, and inner angst. It's OK to be either type or both, but know which it is that your clients are looking for and which that you want to be.

It's also easier to become known for one specific technique such as outdoor or black and white portraits. But in my experience, some clients know that's your specialty and will ask for something else. Know if you're willing to do the something else before they ask.

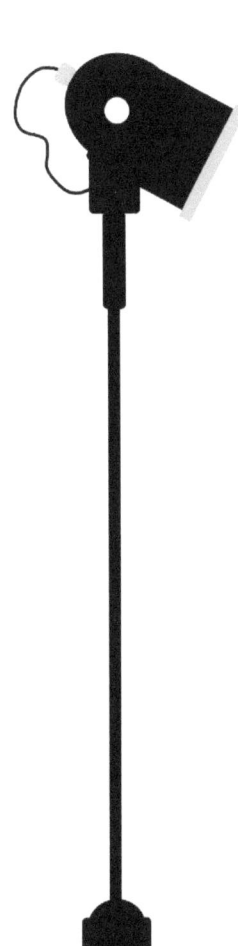

CLOSE UP

In the beginning of my career, I met a photographer who later became a friend. Her name is Sara and what I remember about our first meeting is that she talked about the first time she made a mom cry when the mom saw the portraits of her children that Sarah had taken. She said that is when she considered herself a true pro photographer. This sounded very strange to me at the time. The more she talked, I got it. If the mom cries, you've created images that get an emotional response. From then on, that was the measuring stick for me, too. The first time a mom cried at one of my proof sessions was a great day and I considered myself a professional that day, too. From then on I had a box of tissues on the table at every proof session. Some moms are embarrassed to cry, but their photographer is smiling inside.

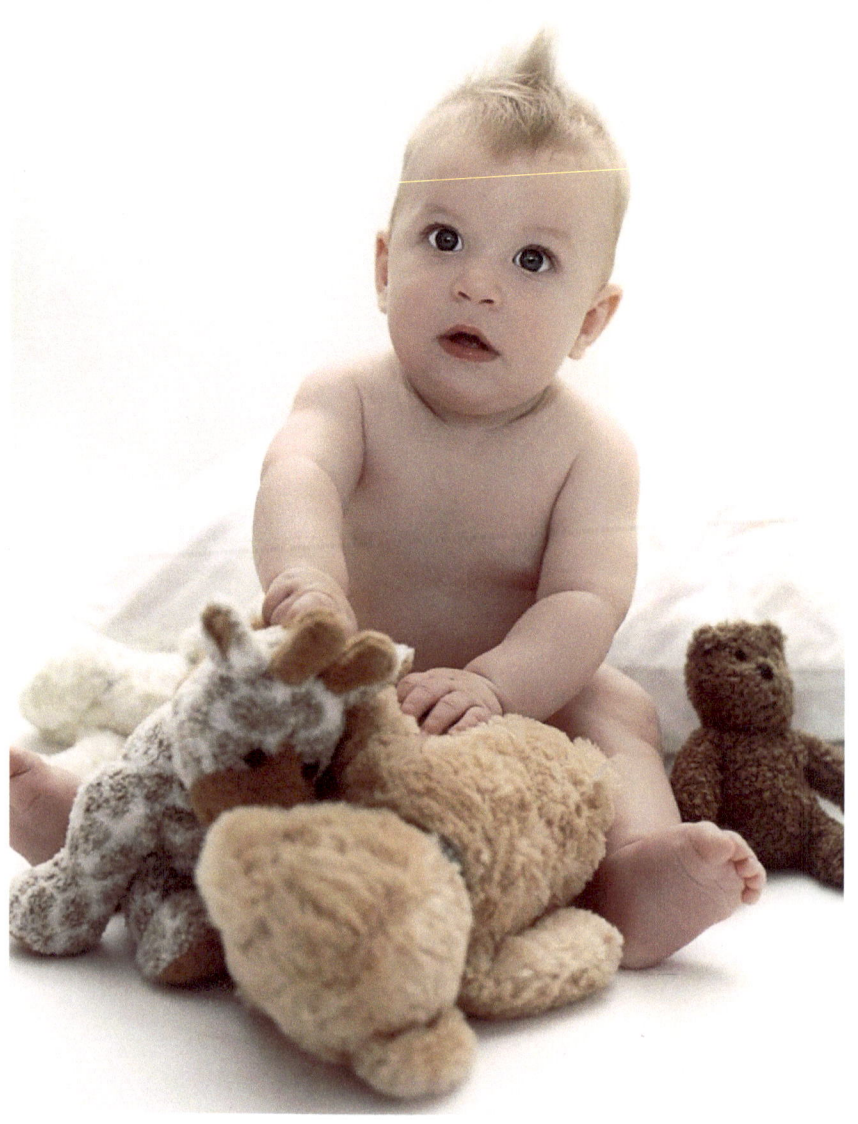

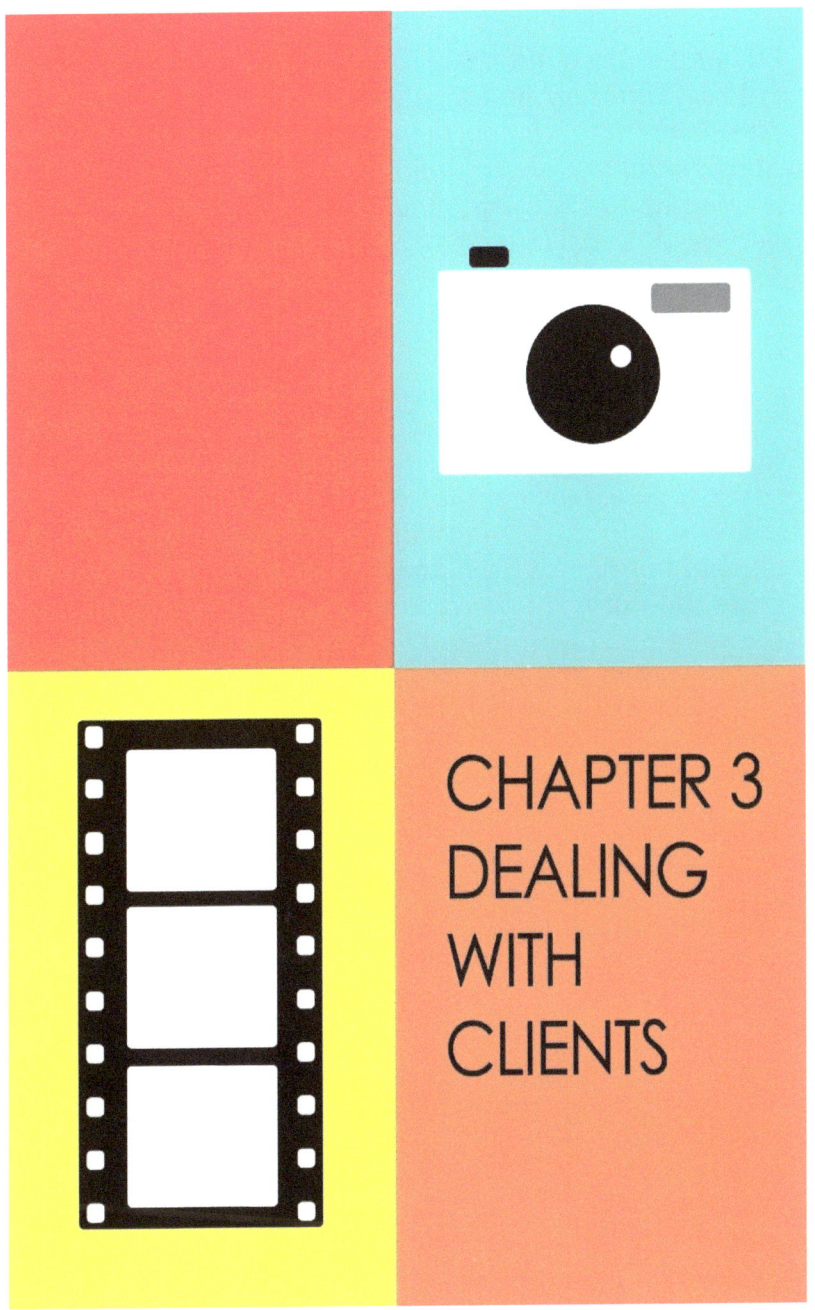

CHAPTER 3
DEALING
WITH
CLIENTS

"When I started out it was a very different time and an entirely different industry. But if there was something I wished I had known then that I know now, it's just how really tough it was to get a toe-hold in the photography industry being a novice. I was so naive, yet in a way that may have actually been more fortunate than not. Had I known then how difficult it was going to be, maybe I would have gone another direction.

Since I am self-taught, I needed to read as much information as I could on photography while at the same time experimenting and trying lots of different ideas to help myself develop my skills. To me, today's students of photography aren't doing that, or in some cases, do not feel it necessary. They're so caught up in the need to learn and do Photoshop and how to use an app to correct mistakes they're not really teaching themselves how to become photographers who do not make mistakes.

Probably the cornerstone of who I am is my ability to shoot a job the first time and make it shine. To create images in every situation asked, that the client loves and can use for whatever purpose they wish."
–David Mecey, Photographer and owner, Mecey Enterprises Intnl., Las Vegas, NV & Los Angeles, CA

Reward Referrals

Reward good clients. I tried to do this, but my system was too complicated. I began a reward program with my high school seniors because I wanted to get more of them. I offered an iPod shuffle or a Macy's gift card to any senior who sent a friend my way. The problem is that this was just too hard to keep track of and some of my seniors fell through the cracks and didn't receive their gift. I also think the gifts were too costly. Not that I thought the referrals were not valuable. As you know, they are extremely valuable. But I was purchasing the items as I needed them and giving the seniors a choice as to what they wanted–the iPod or the gift card, what color iPod, etc. I should have chosen something that I could give to all the seniors and have on hand (like restaurant or iTunes gift cards). It would have been easier to keep track of and keep on top of that way. I would recommend having a reward system, but a simple one.

Teach Your Clients What You Can Do
Your clients don't read *Professional Photographer* or receive the B&H catalog. So they haven't seen everything you have. I assumed that my clients knew what products were out there and what albums looked like. But they didn't know about lay flat and panoramic spreads and dust covers that use their pictures. I assumed they did because I saw them all the time in the publications I was reading, but they had no idea. I should have been better at showing them.

I realized all of this when, a few months after my business was closed I met a woman at a business lunch who breathlessly told everyone at the table how her photographer was so great because she produced the most beautiful album for her daughter's wedding. The photographer arranged several images on some pages, but some single images were spread out over two pages. On some she had used an image from the wedding as a background on the pages. And she used an image from the wedding for the cover! She told us all this as if we had never seen or heard of anything like this before. By now, I was thinking, "Yes, that's what wedding albums look like." And the other people around the table were saying, "Oh," and "Wow." I thought it was odd until I realized that she was amazed by it because SHE had never seen anything like it before. I had seen it my entire career as a photographer in other photographer's studios, magazines, and album catalogs. It never occurred to me that my clients needed to be shown this. They don't see the same things I see. It's so obvious now.

This is again about tooting your own horn. Tell your clients all the cool things you can do with an album. It's so simple, but I didn't see it at the time. I should have done more of it. Value all the things you do and let your clients know about the classes you take and all the work that goes into their images and the products you produce with their images. If you attend a seminar, class or convention, tell them about it through social media or your newsletter. Tell them where you were, what you learned, and how it will impact them in a good way.

References and Testimonials
References and testimonials are so easy to get. All you have to do is ask. These work very well, especially if people see people they know in the testimonials. They are the best way to get word out that your services are valued in your community. Clients will sometimes provide unsolicited testimonials through thank you notes or e-mails. But they don't expect to see their personal correspondence on your website as a testimonial. So ask them if you can use a sentence or two as a testimonial. And ask the clients who don't send thank you notes to provide you with a sentence or two via e-mail.

One very important point about testimonials: Tell your clients where their testimonial will appear and that you will use their name (testimonials without names are cheesy). If you accompany the testimonial with a portrait of a child, use only the client's first name and a last initial or just their first name.

I made the mistake of using a testimonial with a client's full name and town she lived in next to a portrait of her child. Although she was nice about it, she was very upset. This was in the early days of the internet and I hadn't thought this through. I saw her point and took out her last name and town immediately while we were still on the phone together.

Listen to Your Clients
Listen to the client and what they are asking for. In the beginning of my career, a client showed me a space above her fireplace where a horizontal portrait could go, but I only took vertical portraits. Not too bright. Really listen to your client's needs and take some poses that will fit those needs.

Another client I failed to listen to asked about framing. I offered very limited frames—sets of two square frames with white mats. But instead of asking her what she wanted and saying yes to her (I knew a good framer and could have purchased any framing she wanted from him and charged her for the service), I told her I didn't offer frames. I didn't even explore it and I lost out on the cash and the relationship I could have had with her. Not to mention all the good things she might have said about me to her friends about the fact that I offered framing, and went above and beyond for her when she wanted it.

Listen to Yourself

If you have a funny feeling about a client or a situation, listen to that and turn down the job. I did a portrait session in my early career for a woman who wanted pictures of her son as a birthday gift to her husband. I took the pictures and she liked them and ordered some. A couple of days after she picked them up, she called and said she hated them. I was on vacation at the time so I left her a message that I would call her when I got home. But it caused a lot of stress to me knowing this was waiting for me when I got back.

When I returned, I gathered up my courage and called her. She said, oh no, never mind, her husband actually loved the portraits and there was no problem. I was puzzled, but relieved that the situation had resolved itself.

About two years later, she called to tell me her extended family was coming into town and asked me to take family portraits. I was surprised because she had been so unhappy the last time and I felt a little twinge of "Hm . . . should I do this?" I decided that the first time had been a fluke, and I should go ahead and do it. This is the job that turned into the Incredible Expanding Family mentioned earlier.

I think you see what's going to happen here. She hated the pictures and complained about everything. Her son deliberately turned his face away in every family group picture. Then she complained that there weren't any without her son turning his head and did I have any better ones!

I realized I am far from perfect, so I showed the images to another photographer who would not sugar coat anything and would tell me if the pictures stink in no uncertain terms. He didn't see a problem with them.

I should have listened to that feeling I had when I first talked with her about this job and not accepted it. For more on this topic, I highly recommend the book *The Gift of Fear* by Gavin de Becker. It's about listening to your instincts and getting out of dangerous situations before they escalate. It's written for parents to help keep children safe and it's not for the faint of heart. But the information in it will help anyone learn how to read situations and people and avoid bad ones. I had read the book before this incident and I should have listened to my inner voice telling me this was not a good idea. It would have saved me much stress and trouble.

Too Much of a Good Thing
This one is easy and is not something I had to worry about in the film days. When you take 150 digital images in a session, narrow them down to no more than 30 or so, unless you're a wedding photographer. Show only the very best images and don't show ones that are too similar to each other.

Delete What You Don't Need
Clients never, ever, ever come back for more. I really wish someone had told me this at some point in my ten years as a studio owner. Clients often ask at the proof appointment if they can come back and order more later. They say they will. They don't. E.V.E.R.

I knew a photographer who told her clients that once they placed their order, all the images from the session that were not ordered were erased from the computer and they could not order additional poses after that day. I thought this was harsh and didn't adopt this policy.

When clients asked me if they could come back for more, I said, "Sure. I keep them forever." This was equally as bad as erasing them as soon as their bodies cleared the studio door. No one ever came back for more.

I wish I had devised a system for selling more after the initial proof appointment with a middle-of-the-road erasure policy. I could have said that the images are kept for two months, for example. Then at the one month mark, I could have sent a postcard or an e-mail with a reminder that they had one month left.

Shoot Until the Client Goes Home

I missed some great shots because I relaxed and thought we were done. Then the kids started doing something really cute and the camera was off or across the room.

One boy in particular stands out in my mind. He came to me for portraits when he was 12 or so. He lives close, so he walked and arrived without his parents. But they had coached him to be good and do what I said. He's a nice boy so he did. We took outdoor portraits of him in regular clothes and in his soccer uniform with his soccer ball. When we were done (he thought), he began kicking the soccer ball around and balancing it on his head and hitting it with his knees, and other fun stuff. "Hey, where has this been," I asked and kept shooting. Most of the poses his mom purchased were those last poses where he was relaxed and being himself.

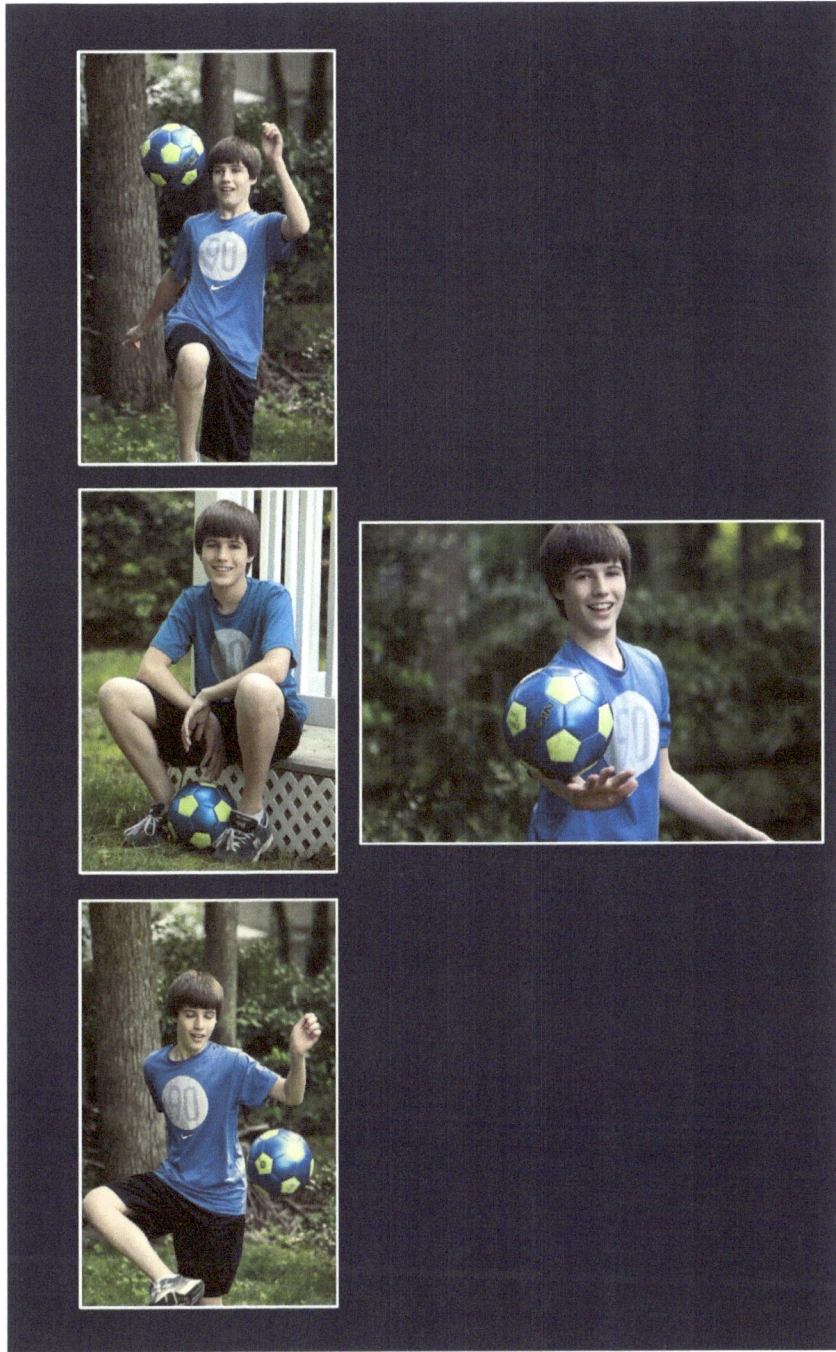

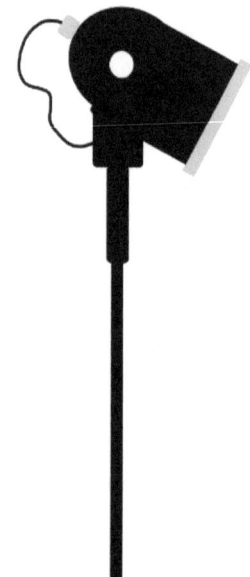

CLOSE UP

Keep shooting and keep your energy up even if it seems like the session is not going well.

I once took portraits of a girl on one of those days I was describing earlier where I rented space and saw several clients in one day. This really cute little girl came in with her mom. They had just come from running errands and the little girl was wearing a denim jumper and a bright magenta shirt underneath. This was an adorable outfit, but on camera, it was too loud and didn't go with the background I had brought. So I kept talking and taking pictures and had the girl play with some props that I had there even though I could see on the screen on my camera that the colors were just awful. When I got back to the studio, I transformed the image to sepia tone to get rid of the clashing colors and immediately had classic beautiful portraits that made the mom cry.

Another time a new mom and dad came in with their baby.

The baby was so good and we got lots of great pictures of her. But I really wanted one with all of them. Being new parents, I'm sure they spent all their energy that morning getting out of the house, so neither parent was prepared to be in the portrait. As most new moms, this mom was wearing sweats. Luckily she had a grey t-shirt on under the sweatshirt, I asked her to take off the sweatshirt and went in really close for the pose. Then I converted it to black and white so the other colors didn't matter.

The dad actually gasped when he saw this portrait at the proof appointment. I could tell he had no idea what the final product would look like until that moment.

I'm not saying stick with a session even if it's all going downhill and the kids are crying. I'm saying if it's a good situation and you can keep going, do until you feel you have some usable stuff and then work on perfecting the images later. Just be sure to take enough that you have some images to work with.

A photographer once told me, "You only need one good portrait for the session to be a success." In this digital age, we forget this, but he's right.

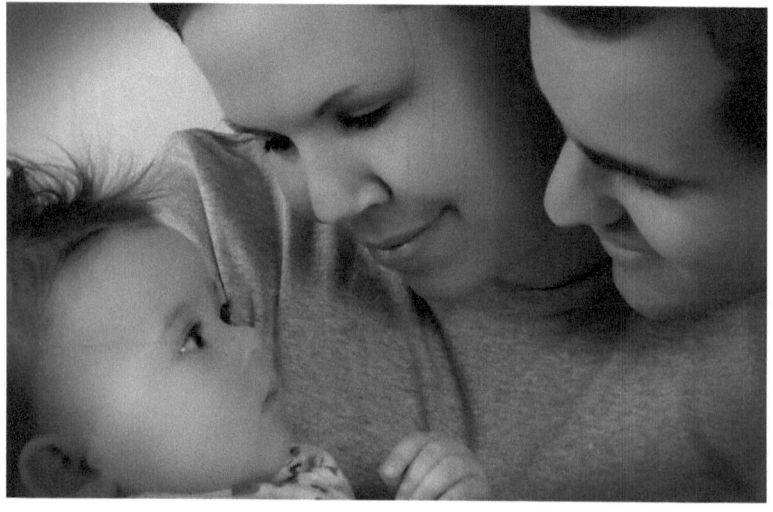

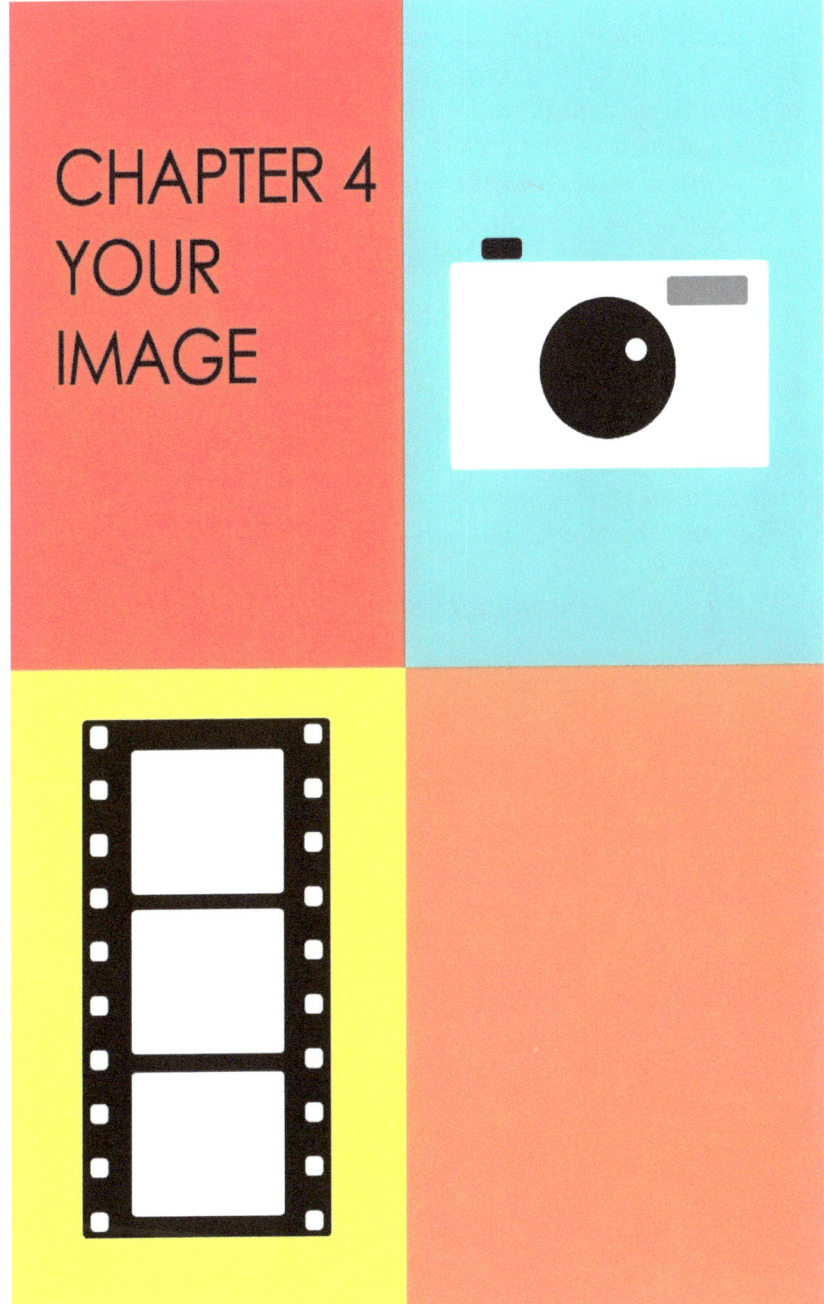

CHAPTER 4
YOUR
IMAGE

"Looking back after 25 years in the photography business, I'm happy with the direction I've taken. There are many decisions made throughout a day, a week or a year, and it is this collection of decisions that creates our path. Know that any one decision will not make or break you. We are constantly adjusting and evaluating our ideas to learn from them and grow our business.

A support group earlier on in my career would have been helpful. Other photographers and entrepreneurs to share ideas and opinions with is a tremendous asset. Even if you just get together to talk and laugh about your day. Find people who share your drive and enthusiasm for business. Look at things from a different perspective as well as enjoying the friendships."
—Patty Sawyer, Star-Light Studios, Laurel, Maryland

As a photographer, you are in the image industry so your own image should be one of professionalism and expertise. When clients first meet you, you want them to trust that you know what you are doing. And fair or unfair, many people decide this based on your outward appearance and the way you talk.

Image Words
Be aware of the words you use when talking with clients. For example, it sounds more professional to use the term "session fee" instead of "sitting fee." Here are some other examples that will make what you do sound as special as it is:

Special	Ordinary
Session	shoot
Artwork	retouching
Image or Portrait	picture or photo
Client	customer

The words you use can elevate the impression clients have of you and your work. It's easy to do and doesn't cost anything. You may have noticed that I used some of the less desirable words in this book (shoot and picture) because I'm talking to other photographers, not a client.

Professional Marketing Materials

Your marketing materials, price lists (or price "menu" if you're talking with a client), business cards, etc. should be printed professionally and should match your website. It actually doesn't cost that much and makes a huge difference in your image. I heard this over and over from others but didn't really believe it and didn't follow the advice. I printed my business cards and brochures on my home printer and they didn't look good at all. Now I believe it. There are lots of places online that will print and mail marketing materials and they make it easy to lay them out and get them all to match. My favorite places for things like this (once I decided to follow the advice I was given) were Vistaprint.com and a local printer in my town with a good reputation and good prices.

Let Your Clothes Make an Impact

Dress up to meet clients. I know that people don't like to dress up anymore, and I'm not saying to spend a lot of money on designer outfits, but have clean clothes and shoes that aren't sneakers and be groomed and look neat. If you don't look pulled together, clients won't trust you to pull a wedding album together. I did many outdoor sessions in my business and I did not dress up for those since I would often kneel or lay on the ground to get the portraits. But for my first meeting with a client, I would dress neatly. If you look like you've just returned from running errands, you're probably not looking your professional best and the client may feel like you're not taking them seriously.

Artists sometimes think they can get away with not dressing properly because they are artists and, as such, can dress however they want. And some can. But keep in mind that this is also a business. Your clients are not artists and they want to feel that you have everything under control. The way you dress can telegraph that.

Packaging

Just as the way you dress says a lot about you, your packaging says a lot about your product inside. There's no need to spend top dollar to have top-of-the-line packaging, but it makes a better impression if it matches your other marketing materials and looks organized. It also makes it fun for the client to go home and unwrap the items. My friends at Starlight Studios in Maryland deliver orders in white boxes placed in gold paper bags with handles and white tissue paper with gold stars. It matches their name and looks sparkly and fun.

My studio placed the prints in a black folder made especially for photos (available online). The folder was wrapped in tissue paper that was the same colors as my logo–lime green, purple, and turquoise–and the bundle went into a clear plastic bag with handles. There was a 4x6 window on the front in which the client's favorite photo from the session was placed. Clients' eyes lit up when they saw their bags waiting for them.

CLOSE UP

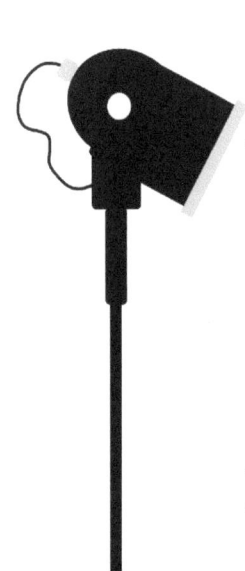

This is a personal pet peeve, so I'll get on my soapbox for a minute. No, you won't go out of business if you don't follow this advice, I simply want to vent. For Pete's sake, put a sample of your work on your business card! When I first started out in the business, a photo on a business card was rarely seen as it was difficult and expensive to get one on a card. Today, with digital printing and myriad online printers to choose from, a photo YOU took is a MUST for your business card. I don't care if it's matte, glossy, full bleed–just have one there and preferably not of yourself. Have one of yourself on your website, yes, but not your card. Your card is an advertisement for your work, so it's best to show it.

The only exception to this would be if you have an extremely unique or clever card that can't accept a photo, like an example I saw online once. It was a business card made out of frosted plastic and it had markings along the bottom and a crosshairs in the middle so that it looked like a camera's viewfinder. The photographer's name, number, and website were on it as well. Very, very clever.

Hindsight is f/20

CHAPTER 5
THINGS I
DIDN'T DO
BUT WISH I
HAD

"Experience is the name everyone gives to their mistakes."
—Oscar Wilde

When I had my business, I paid attention to people and publications and I got lots of good ideas. Here are some that I wished I had followed up on.

Portrait session clothing color cards. I saw this in a magazine article somewhere and loved it. The photographer created post cards that showed three or four colors that go well together as clothing for portraits and had a portrait of a family wearing those colors on the card. It was genius. I had many conversations with families about what to wear and these would have made the process easy for me and the client would have appreciated it too. I just never got around to creating them.

Sell Albums. I had a choice of two albums for seniors and they were both small. I wish I had offered a larger variety. I thought because they were sold so many places and they were so popular, they were boring and people weren't interested. But they are popular for a reason! I should have jumped on that band wagon and ridden it to the bank.

Move to projected proofs earlier. For a while I was showing proofs on my computer, but the orders were for small prints. Once I moved to projected images, the client wanted the finished product to be as big as the projection, so the orders were for larger prints. I heard this advice for years before I took it and wish I had done it earlier.

Offer affordable digital files. This was a new thing

when I was a photographer. I was so afraid of clients using the images to create their own prints, I charged a lot for the files. Then I realized clients don't generally print images. They want to share them with family and friends online. Once I began selling low-resolution digital files on a thumb drive to post on social media, people began purchasing them.

Offer frames. If you talk to enough photographers, you'll hear both pros and cons about offering frames. I never wanted to get into the framing business and didn't have room for a framing corner or the patience to help clients choose the perfect frame and mat. What I wish I had done is offered a limited line. For example, black, white or wood frames with black or white mats would have been a good, simple way to offer frames. I did offer a set of two black square frames with white mats, but the square mat opening made it difficult to find images to fit there and wasn't good for parents with three children. I limited my offerings too much.

Hire an accountant. I am embarrassed to say that I didn't have a handle on how much my images were really costing me to produce. I also was not that organized with regard to inventory and keeping track of credit card fees. It would have helped me immensely to know how much money I really had coming in and going out. I'm not good with numbers and also did not have time to do my own accounting, so I'm sure I was losing money on some products and not charging enough for some items.

Hire a sales person. I'm terrible at sales. I don't like to sell and I'm bad at pointing out all the things I did for a client to make their images perfect. A sales person has no personal feelings toward a client the way I do because I photographed them. A sales person has no problem telling the client how much work went into their images and how special they are and how much they will be worth years from now. I should have seen it and hired that person. I even know who it should have been.

Use a drawing tablet. This is a flat pad like a mouse pad with a virtual pen instead of a mouse that allows you to retouch very precisely. When I was a photographer, Wacom was pretty much the only company that offered them and they were pricy, so I never owned one. These days, lots of companies make them and some are better than others. Do a Google search for "Drawing Tablet" and you'll have a choice of quite a few. Most have reviews so you can see which ones people like using the most. So if you want to try one, they are more affordable now and much easier to use for retouching than a mouse.

Have sample sizes. A photographer I know had the same portrait on his studio wall in sizes from 8x10 up to 20x24. He hung them in a line on the wall opposite the area where proof appointments were conducted. When clients sat there and looked at those portraits on the wall, the 8x10 looked tiny. It was a fantastic way to sell larger sizes. I resisted doing this because of the cost, but in the end it cost me in sales of larger prints because I didn't do it.

CLOSE UP

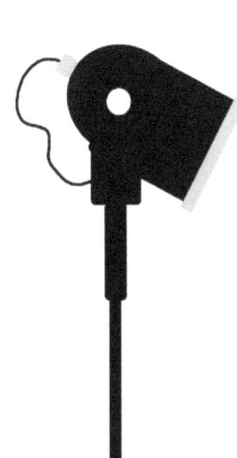

One of my clients called in November to schedule her daughter's senior portrait session for January. We talked about what she wanted and she wanted studio portraits with outfit changes and also outdoor portraits. She also said, "I would like some pictures of her in the snow." We live in Maryland and sometimes entire winters go by without any snow, so I said, "OK. We can certainly do that if it snows that day . . ." and wondered how she thought I might make it snow for the session. When she arrived it was a cold January day. We took the studio portraits and then decided to move outside. When we looked out the window, it was snowing! It had been snowing for a while and the ground was covered. We got very lucky that day and I learned that there is something to be said for putting your wishes out to the universe.

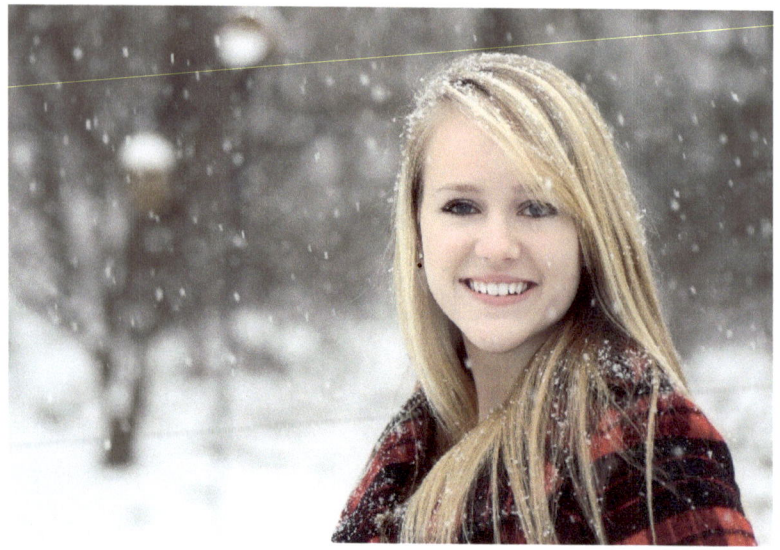

CHAPTER 6
EQUIPMENT
AND
SOFTWARE

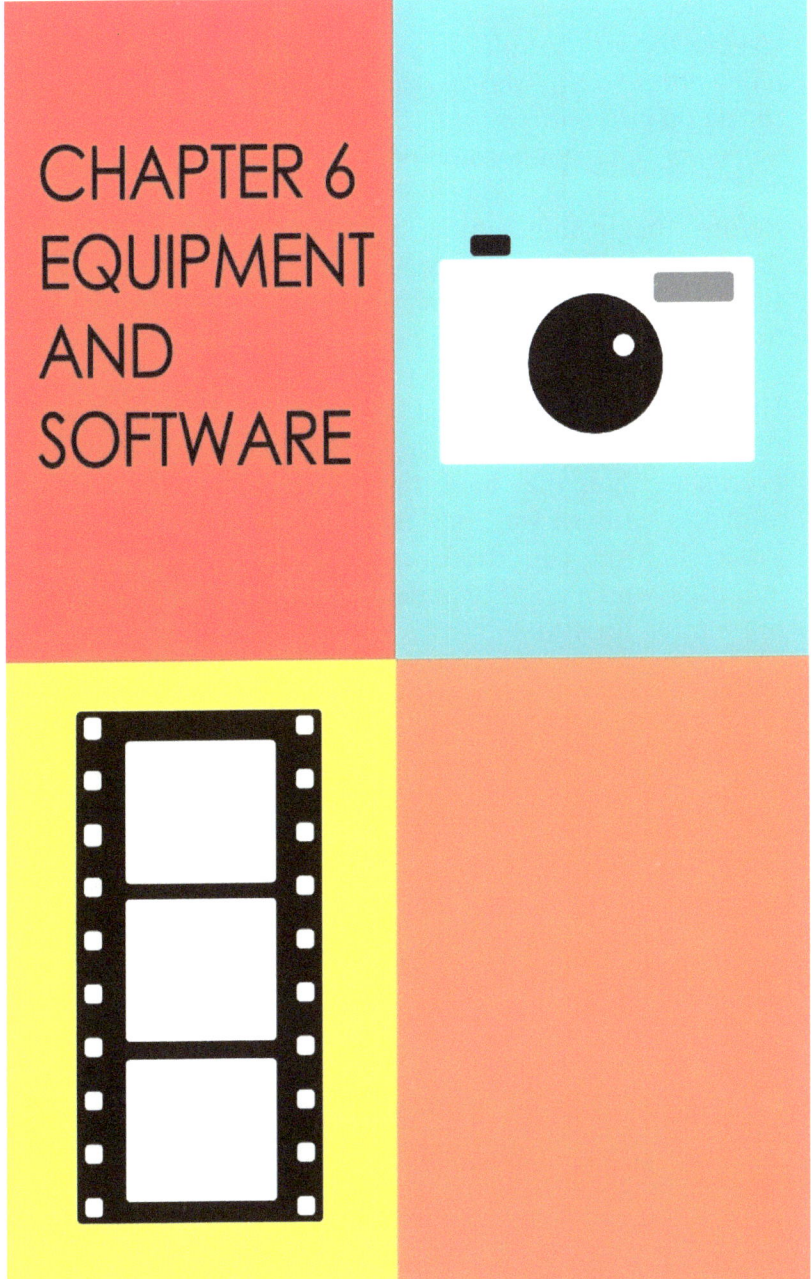

"Never forget that all the great photographs in history were made with more primitive camera equipment than you currently own."
—Brooks Jensen, photographer and editor of LensWork

Before I begin this section I want to make it clear that I do not work for any of these companies. They are things I really used in my business that made life easier. Also, I never owned the best, most expensive camera available.

Have the best equipment you need for the specific things you do. For example, if you are shooting sports events for a living, have the best zoom lens you can afford, a camera that has burst mode and can handle lots of lighting conditions, can handle rainy conditions and dust, and a good tripod. A really great macro lens is not a must for you.

Photoshop Elements. As stated earlier, I'm not much of a technical person, so the fact that Elements let me do everything I wanted with regard to retouching, filters, vignettes, cropping, correcting color, and all the things I needed to do, it was just right for me. It was not as pricy as the full version of Photoshop and it didn't take up as much memory on my computer. You may find that you need the full version. Research it first to make sure before you spend the big bucks on the full version.

ProSelect by TimeExposure. I really love this proofing software. It allows you to place the images in a folder and look at them one by one, all at once, or in a slideshow. You can show images in original form, black and white or sepia with the click of a button. You can crop, lay out albums, see what they look like framed, and even see what they would look like on your client's wall in the size they order. It allows you to put the images in Yes, Maybe and No piles which makes it easy to narrow them down with your client. I'm sure by now it does even more. This is such a fun program and it makes proof appointments easy.

Portrait Professional. This oh-so-easy-to-use software works on the basis of a beauty grid and the notion that the more symmetrical a face is, the more beautiful we find it. It re-sculpts a person's face very slightly or a lot depending on what level you have it set for to make the face perfectly symmetrical. You can brighten eyes (which I think this program does exceptionally well), add vibrancy to hair, whiten teeth, add catch lights to eyes, and so much more I can't mention it all. My favorite part of this program is that as long as you don't overdo it, it makes people look better but so subtly that they still look like themselves. Clients look at the portraits and see themselves, but better, and don't know that anything has changed.

Bokeh plug-in by Alien Skin. This is a plug in that allows you to make a portion of a portrait blurry and you can choose the intensity of the blur. It also allows you to create vignettes in colors as well as black and white and you choose the intensity and the width of the vignette. I used this all the time. As with retouching, I went easy on it and my favorite effect was to slightly darken the corners of portraits. It's a professional touch that puts more emphasis on the subject's face.

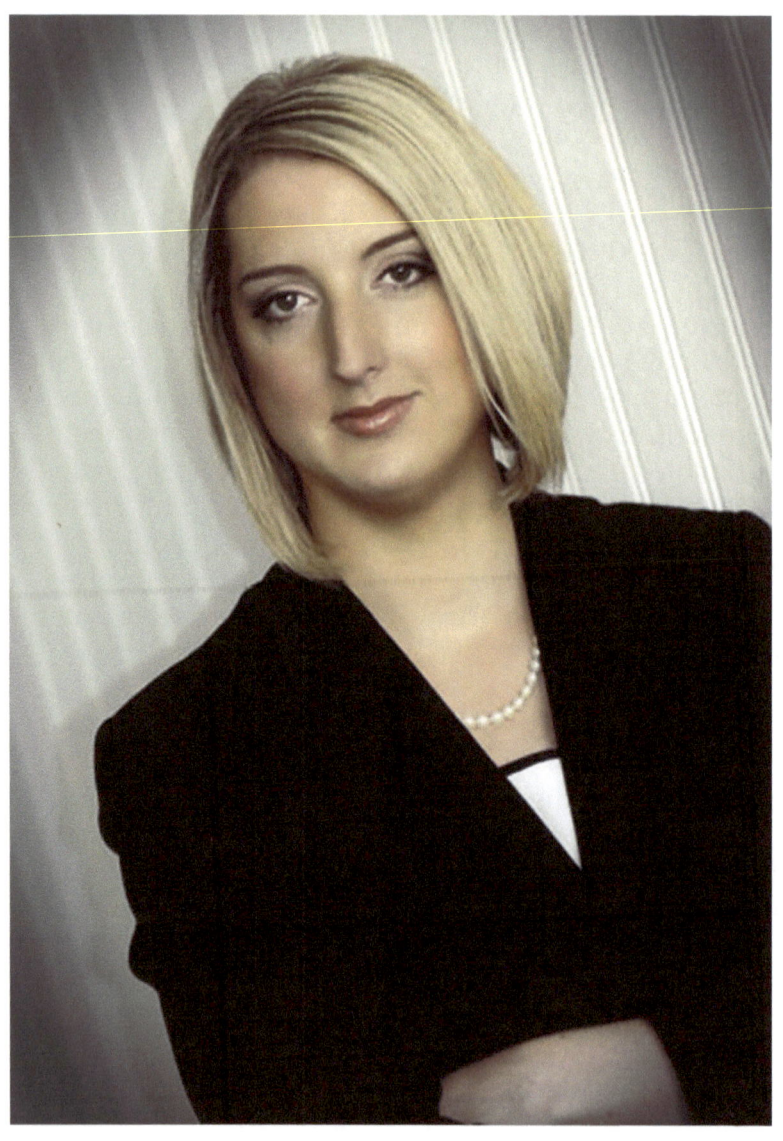

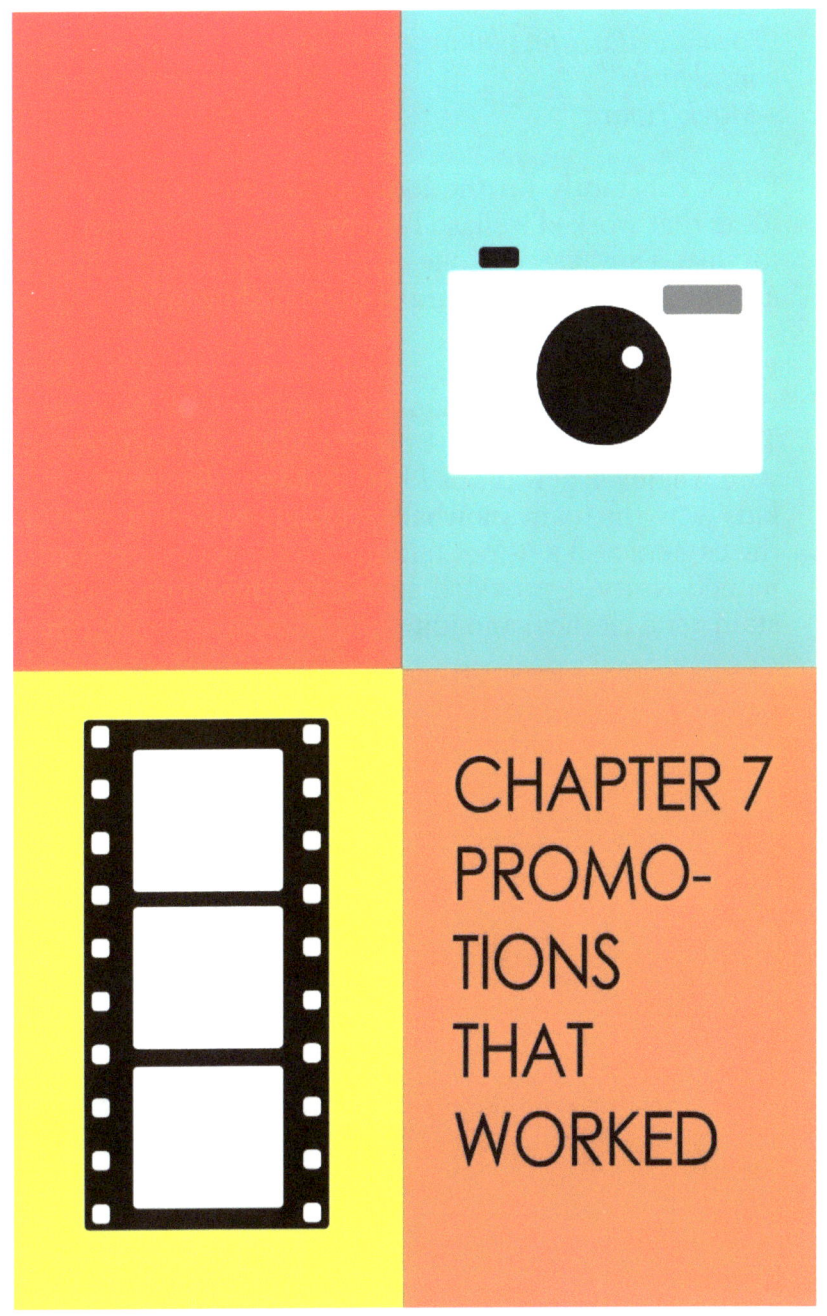

CHAPTER 7
PROMO-
TIONS
THAT
WORKED

"To succeed in life, you need two things: ignorance and confidence."
—Mark Twain

I was constantly on the lookout for event and promo ideas that worked well, so here are the ones that worked for me. They are the ones that people would call me about and say, "Are you going to do that again?"

Holiday Sessions. They would have worked if I had stuck with them and changed the date (see Page 22). These were a lot of fun. I decorated the room I rented with whatever new props I had that year. Favorites with kids were the foam snowballs which they could throw at the camera and a 3-foot tall nutcracker we very cleverly named Nutty. I provided snacks (nothing chocolate to stain good clothes) and juice and also played some fun

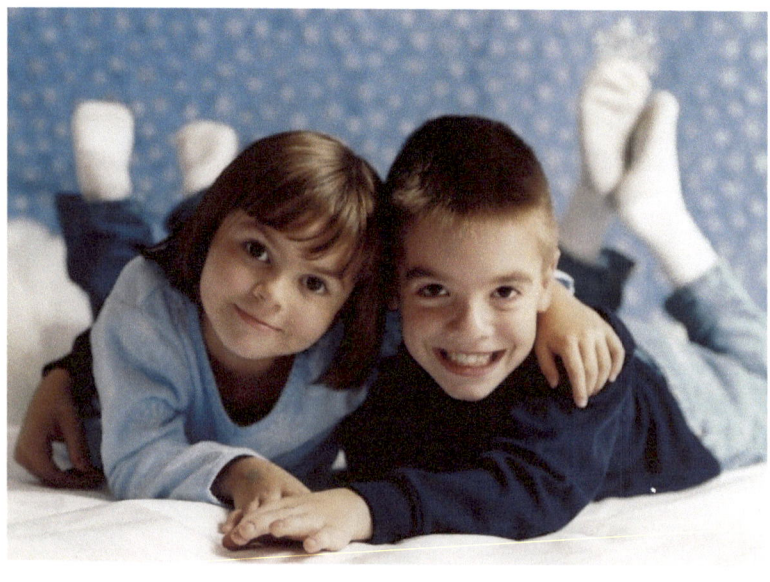

Christmas music. One year the background was blue fabric with silver sparkly snowflakes. Another time it was plain white which made the Christmas outfit colors pop.

Park Sessions. These were always popular. I did them in the spring and fall when the parks were at their prettiest. Clients like being outside at those times too. I chose parks with special features such as a gazebo, waterfall, or lots of flowering bushes. Just a hint on taking outdoor photos around flowers: portraits look better when the subject is not posed right next to the flowers. Lots of colorful flowers look great as a blur in the background of a portrait.

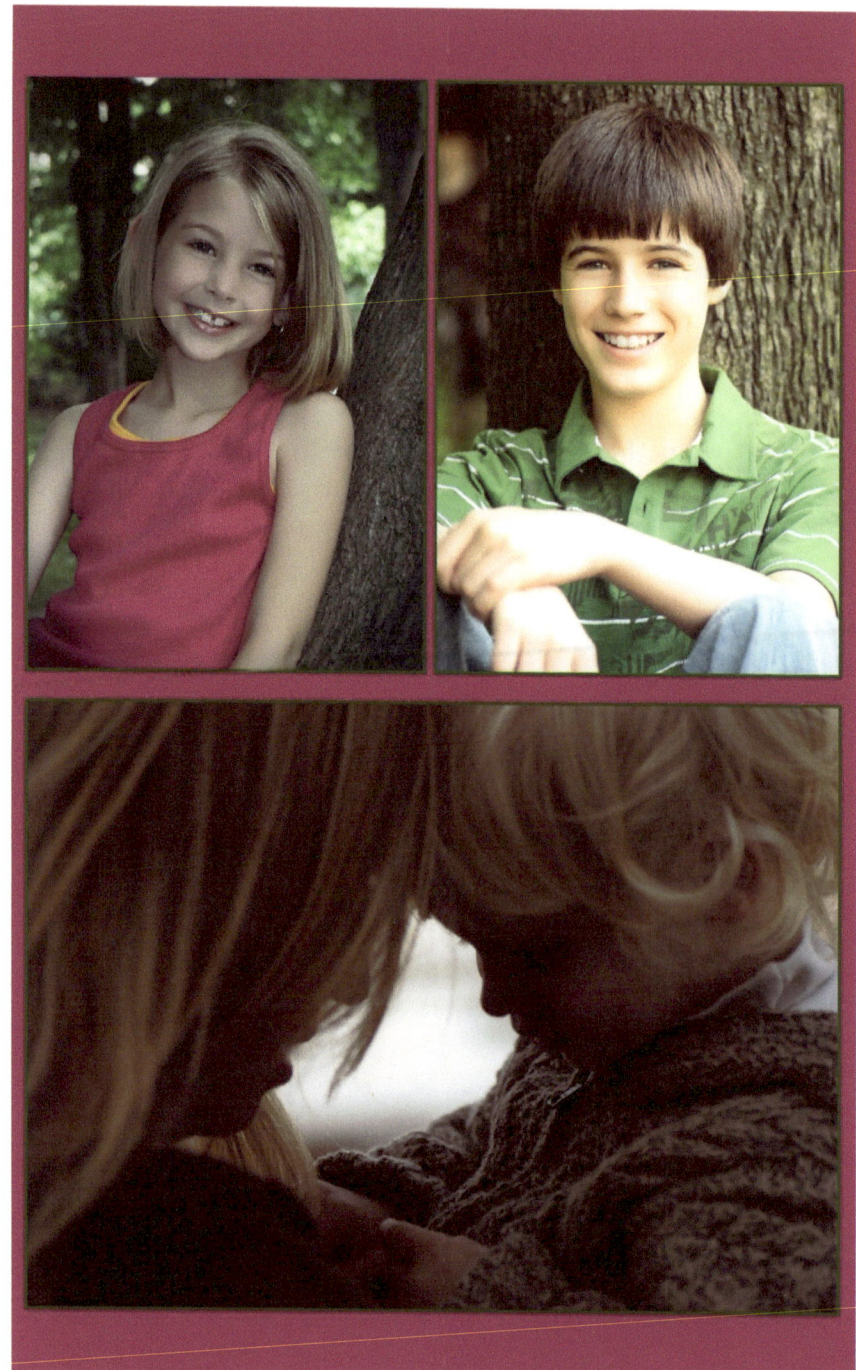

Bunny Sessions. The Bunny Session was the most work and the most popular. One year, a friend who owns an antique store housed in a converted huge, old church wanted to get people into her store in the spring, so we decided to do a spring session in the store. She cleared out an entire room for me to use for the session so I could set up my equipment.

I contacted a local woman who breeds and keeps rabbits. I asked her if I could borrow a litter of baby bunnies for a photography session. I wanted to make sure the bunnies would not be bothered by the flash and that having kids holding them all day would not upset them. She assured me that none of this would bother them.

I visited her farm when the bunnies were babies and she gave me a choice of which litter to take for the day (they had to be returned to the mother by evening). I chose a litter that had one each of white, brown, black, and spotted.

My daughter was the bunny handler for the day and she was about 10 so that fit in perfectly with what she wanted to do that day. A friend who knew the rabbit breeder came along to help and keep an eye on things.

The kids who came loved the fact that there were live bunnies hopping around and that they could hold them. In case you're wondering, yes we cleaned up some bunny poop that day, but it's neat little pellets, so it's easy to clean up. I also used a white background made of plastic so it was easy to spray with cleaner and wipe off. And, yes, in one of the portraits I retouched out some bunny poop. We were careful not to let the kids get to it. Some clients asked if I could add baby chicks to the session the next year.

Because of the timing of when baby bunnies are born and ready to be handled, the session was right before Easter and the portraits were not ready by Easter, but I let all of my clients know that up front.

Clients who attended that session and even ones who could not make it called me as early as the next winter to see if I was going to do that session again.

It was a lot of extra work to pick up live animals and have them back by the end of the day in addition to setting up and breaking down all my equipment but it was worth it to get those pictures of kids with bunnies.

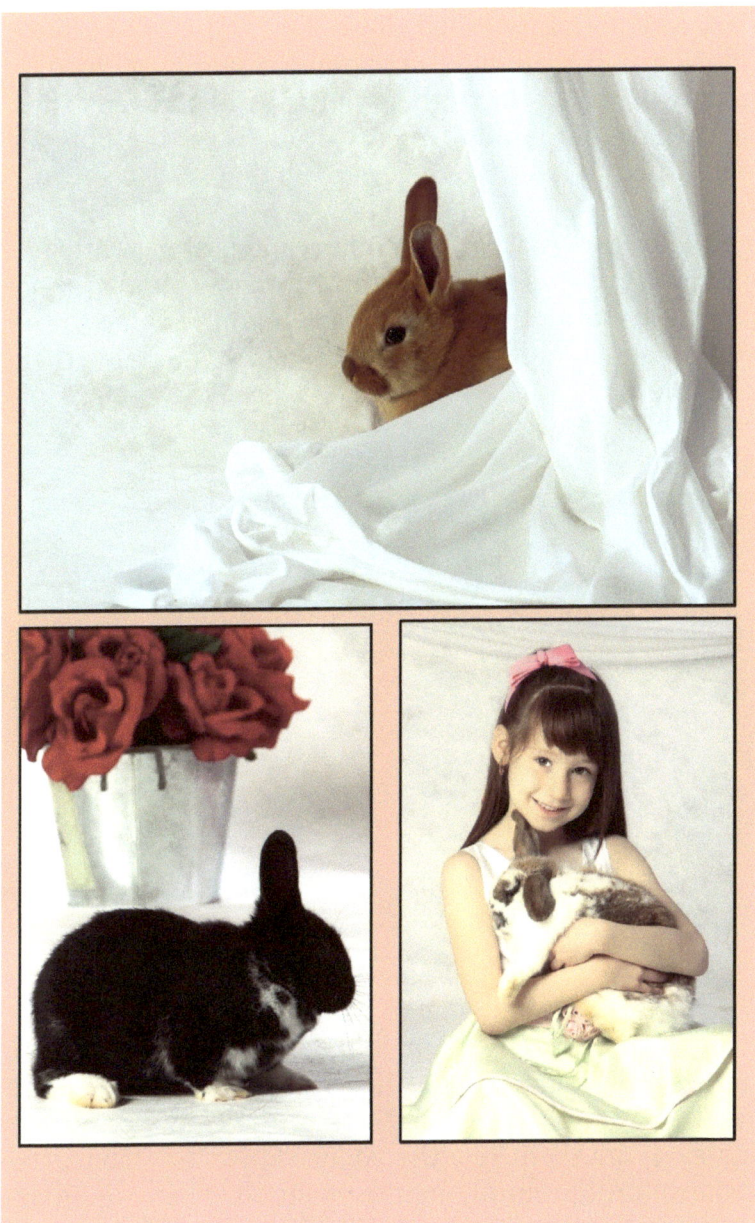

Pick and Click. I called these Pick and Click because different family units of an extended family could pick their own day to have their portrait taken even when more than one family was involved. Then the portrait was crafted to look like they were all there together.

In the picture below, a brother and sister wanted a portrait of themselves and their families to give their parents as an anniversary gift. Each family came to the studio on a different day to accommodate their schedule.

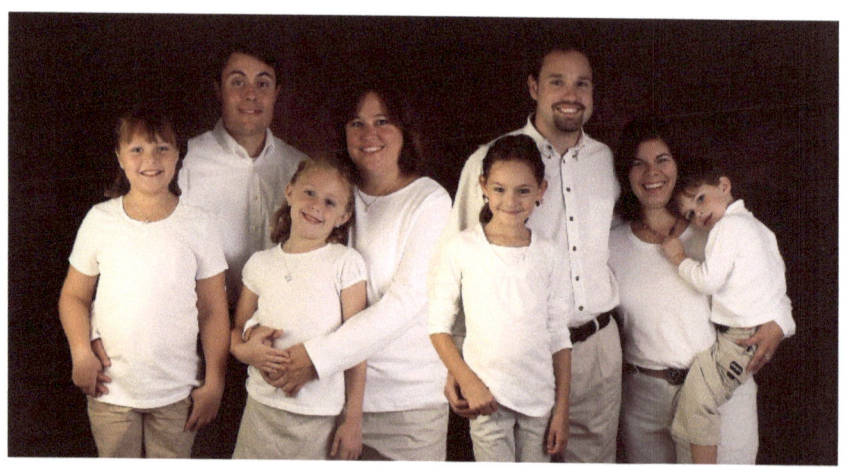

When the first family came in, I marked with tape on the floor where my light stands and tripod were. I marked with tape on the light stands how high they were. I wrote down the settings of the camera and the lights. I marked on the floor how far from the background the family members stood. Then when the next family came in I set everything **exactly** the same as when the first family was there. The families even came for their proof appointments separately.

Then each family's favorite pose was merged into one portrait with Photoshop Elements. The family loved it because they didn't have to plan around each others' schedules. The portrait also was wider than a regular portrait and they liked the larger size since the portrait was a gift to go over the fireplace in their parents' home.

For the second type of Pick and Click, each family member's portrait was taken separately against a white background. I made sure none of them stood in the same pose. This portrait is very long and narrow. The client had it professionally framed and hung it over the fireplace, where it still hangs today.

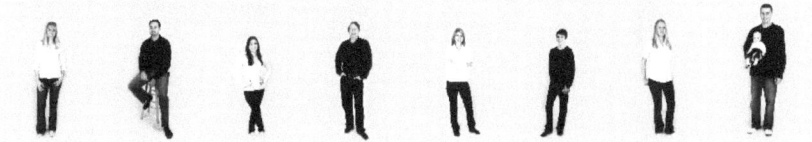

Hindsight is f/20

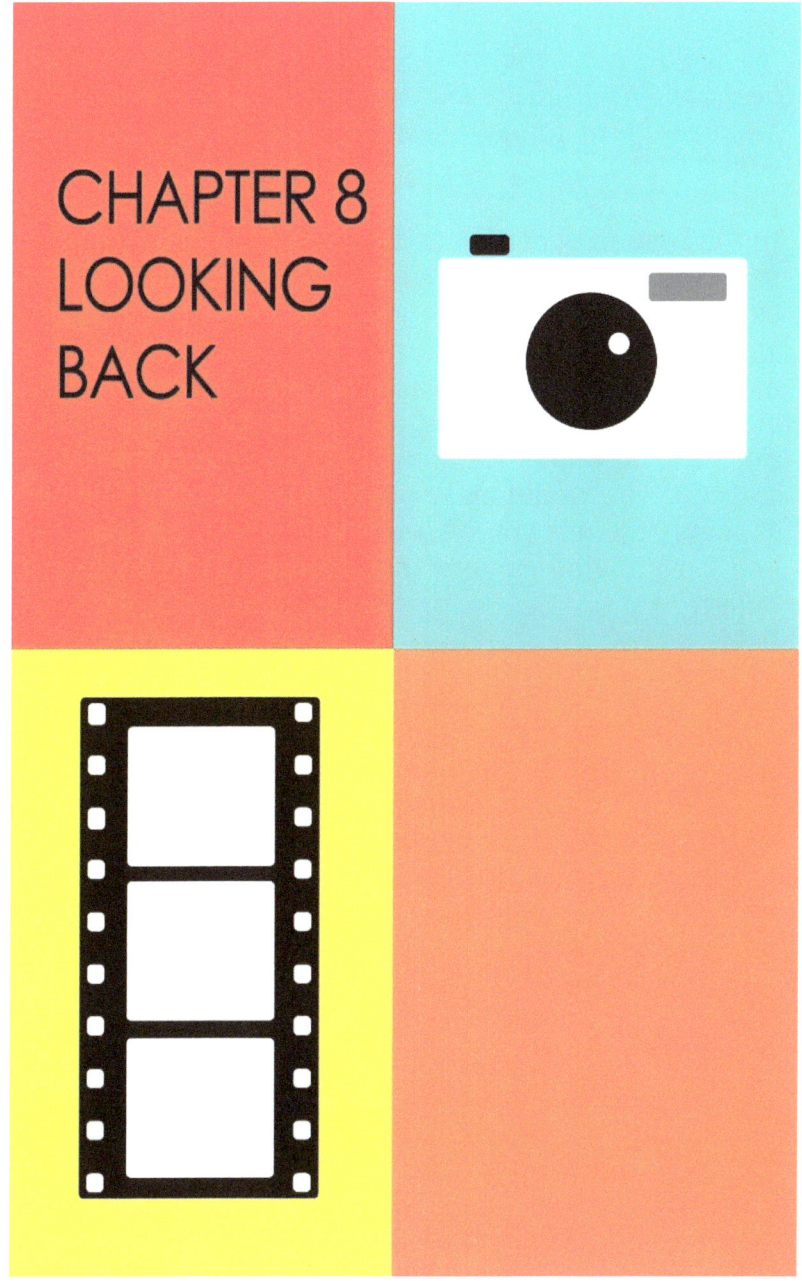

CHAPTER 8
LOOKING
BACK

"May you have the hindsight to know where you've been, The foresight to know where you are going, And the insight to know when you have gone too far"
—*Irish Blessing*

In the beginning of my business, only one photographer in the association I belonged to used a digital camera. Over the next four or five years, everyone went digital and it was a HUGE learning curve. And the software companies and labs and camera manufacturers learned along with us. It was kind of a mess really. You would purchase a digital camera and three months later, someone else would make one that was so much better, suddenly the one you owned was obsolete. I remember one early digital camera that used a CD to write the images to.

The first digital camera I owned had a lag time of about 5 seconds before I could take another picture. I only used it for about six months until a better one came out.

Then the consumer cameras began going digital and coming down in price and clients began purchasing the same camera I used (or a newer one). Then the economy tanked. By the end it was really not a good situation all the way around. But I certainly can't blame the demise of my business all on that.

I didn't work with other photographers first. I just learned photography and started a business. People called me a mom with a camera. And I admit I could have learned a lot from working with another photographer first instead of just jumping in cold. I clearly did some things wrong in my business. The frustrating thing about it is that at the time, I couldn't see what I was doing wrong. I can only see it now.

But I did some things right and I met a lot of great people. I never had anyone not pay or write a bad check. I only had two clients who were ever unhappy with the work. I am still friends with many of my clients. Photography is a very personal business and it's impossible to treat clients as simple business transactions.

Some clients came back to me year after year for their Christmas card pictures, so I saw their kids grow up. Many of my friends turned into clients. I was very fortunate in my business in that it was mostly a positive experience. And I have thousands of great, professional portraits of my own family members.

I photographed a cookbook and, yes, we got to eat the food. I got back stage at local concerts, plays, and sports events. I photographed entire staffs at corporations. I photographed authors for book jackets and local politicians.

I heard fun, happy, and heartbreaking stories from clients. I was there at the beginning of the forming of companies. I was on the board of the moms association. I had some really wacky clients. I gave away some free stuff to people who I felt needed a hand and once I got a nice hefty tip from a client. I started another company called Photo Finish to help people turn their own photos into fun stuff. I earned extra money doing stock photography. I became a Certified Professional Photographer. I was hired long distance by the British magazine *Engineering and Technology* to take photos of an executive they were writing about.

My portraits of business people are on books, magazine articles, websites, business cards, brochures, and CD cases. I spoke at camera clubs. I started a photographers' group. I got to hold and photograph an Emmy award.

I had a ball.

I know you will too and I hope I've provided you with some lessons that were hard-learned so that you won't have to go through it the way I did.

ACKNOWLEDGEMENTS

Thanks to my fabulous clients who agreed to have their portraits in this book. I promised not to use your names, so you know who you are.

Many thanks to Kayle Simon for her professional guidance and for making me look professional, too.

Thanks to Peggy Johnson for constant encouragement and being as excited about this book as I am.

Patty and Daniel, there are several projects I could not have pulled off without your help. Thanks for letting me spend hours at your studio watching and learning and for feeding me, too.

Most of all, thanks to my family–the ones I live with and the ones far away–who are always supportive of anything I do.

www.ingramcontent.com/pod-product-compliance
Lightning Source LLC
Chambersburg PA
CBHW040906180526
45159CB00010BA/2943